GENEROSITY RULES!

GENEROSITY RULES!

A GUIDEBOOK TO GIVING

CLAIRE GAUDIANI
With David Burnett

iUniverse, Inc.
New York Lincoln Shanghai

GENEROSITY RULES!
A GUIDEBOOK TO GIVING

Copyright © 2007 by Claire L. Gaudiani

iUniverse books may be ordered through booksellers or by contacting:

iUniverse
2021 Pine Lake Road, Suite 100
Lincoln, NE 68512
www.iuniverse.com
1-800-Authors (1-800-288-4677)

Because of the dynamic nature of the Internet, any Web addresses or links contained in this book may have changed since publication and may no longer be valid.

The views expressed in this work are solely those of the author and do not necessarily reflect the views of the publisher, and the publisher hereby disclaims any responsibility for them.

ISBN: 978-0-595-47128-7 (pbk)

ISBN: 978-0-595-91409-8 (ebk)

Printed in the United States of America

CONTENTS

PREFACE

If you grew up here in America and are reading *Generosity Rules!*, I know a couple of things about you already. Chances are you enjoy a reasonable level of comfort in life. You are also, I feel confident, a beneficiary of the generosity of your fellow citizens.

How can I be so sure about this, when I really don't know anything about you or your background? Because we Americans have all benefited, every one of us, from our national tradition of generosity. We have each received gifts of time or money from our fellow citizens that have contributed to the prosperity you and I enjoy today.

This story has inspired me and I hope it will inspire you. I spent thirteen years as a college president. As part of my responsibilities, I asked many people to be generous to the college. And they were. We raised over one hundred fifty million dollars dollars! When I stepped down, I wanted to learn more about philanthropy. So I researched and wrote a book called *The Greater Good* about the economic and social history of American giving. I did learn a lot, and I developed a deeper appreciation for my own good fortune. My husband, David, and I both went to wonderful colleges on scholarships given by donors we didn't even know. David's grandmother, who was widowed in 1917, supported her family with the help of the Detroit Women's Exchange, part of a great citizen philanthropic program of the 20th century.

I concluded in *The Greater Good* that "Americans are not generous because we are rich. We are rich because we are generous." This is a pretty radical idea, and I've now spent several years traveling the country to tell the story. The response from audiences large and small, in big cities and small towns, has been enthusiastic. People are fascinated by the stories of American givers and the benefits produced by their generosity.

Many listeners have asked for a 'handbook' that outlines the big ideas in *The Greater Good*. So I decided to write *Generosity Rules!* It is a fast-paced overview of America's number one value, citizen generosity. It shows the economic, as well as the social, importance of generosity. It concludes with some 'rules' for how you can ensure the continuation of this important tradition across our nation. I hope you are inspired to join in.

INTRODUCTION

Do you have a pension fund for your retirement? Is it diversified? Have you ever taken an anti-biotic? Or had an MRI? Ever visit the local art or history museum? These are just a few random examples of the gifts we enjoy every day, thanks to generous citizens. Some of these givers were rich (as rich as Rockefeller, as the song goes) and others gave only a dime or two (ninety percent of U.S. citizens contributed a total of four billion dimes to the Mother's March Against Polio in the 1940's and 50's).

The story of generosity is full of surprises. America is a nation of givers and we are better off, individually and collectively, because of it. Citizen generosity is our most widely shared value. Eighty nine percent of Americans voluntarily give money away to others each year, more than eat fast food, watch the Superbowl or vote. We are the most generous nation on earth. Individual citizens give about one and one half percent of our Gross Domestic Product (total of all goods and services produced each year) to various causes. In 2006, this amounted to about two hundred thirty billion dollars.

This is *not* money donated by corporations or by large foundations such as Ford, Rockefeller or Gates. It is money regular citizens contribute from their paychecks and savings accounts to fund medical research, soup kitchens, church missions, little league fields, and local theater groups. No other citizens in the world even come close to these numbers, either as a percentage of GDP or in absolute dollars.

The size of the numbers doesn't really matter, of course. It is the spirit of generosity that makes us wealthy. Contributions create a special asset. They fund our 'non-profit', or as I prefer, our 'social profit' sector. This sector provides much of the energy and creativity that keeps our nation growing. The 'can-do' spirit of citizen problem-solvers is our core strength. Local solutions, fueled by donated money, often become the basis for larger government programs after the smaller experiments are proven to work. We have seen this pattern over and over again throughout our history. College scholarships, the criminalization of drunk driving, personal retirement funds, and support for basic scientific research are just a few examples. These and many other programs were started by local people using their own money to improve the greater good. Only decades, and in some cases centuries, later did the government get involved.

Citizen investment has been remarkably consistent over the centuries. This is what has created our dependable tradition. We do respond when a crisis occurs, especially the terrible natural disasters that happen all too frequently. We need to open up our hearts and our wallets in these moments, and we do! But this kind of charity is not what defines our giving. It is not what has built our nation. It is our willingness, day in and day out, to invest in each other and in our communities. We identify a greater good and we go to work to make the vision a reality. We embrace improvement; home improvement, self improvement, community improvement. This attitude, supported by generous citizens, has built the prosperity we enjoy today.

Our market-based economic system is very good at accumulating capital and building wealth. Business entrepreneurs whose names you know, such as Ford, Carnegie, Mellon, and Vanderbilt, put this new system to work during the Industrial Revolution of the late 19th century. They created their fortunes and our modern nation in the process. They also created a highly unequal distribution of wealth. Happily for our nation, social entrepreneurs were investing time and money for social profit in parallel with the efforts of the so-called 'robber barons.' We will meet the builders of the Women's Exchanges, the Settlement Houses, the higher education institutions, and the other elements of our social fabric in coming chapters. Eventually, many of the barons gave back large portions of their fortunes, building museums, churches, foundations, parks and performance spaces that all citizens could enjoy. America prospered as capitalism and civil society grew together.

We enjoy a 'trifecta' of capitalism, democracy, and social profit investment in America. Our system has built a remarkably stable society that has grown consistently over centuries. Sometimes we have to stop for a moment to reflect on our progress. When our country was founded, the idea of human 'progress', meaning upward social and economic mobility for large numbers of people, was little more than a theory. The European thinkers who advanced such ideas frequently had to duck for cover lest the local monarch put an end to their misguided musings. Today we assume that each generation will fare better than the previous one, and when that didn't happen (only once) following the Great Depression, Americans expressed their upset with a radical rethinking of the role of government.

This experience is very important today as we consider how to manage the wealth we have accumulated in our nation. *Generosity Rules!* summarizes how generosity works for the social and economic benefit of our communities. Generosity is generative. It produces social profit, including increased generosity. This cycle of growth has been repeated millions of times over the history of our country. Each cycle sustains the next and inspires more generosity.

Generosity in America is not one check for one crisis. It is a way of living. Stephen Jay Gould[1] has the right idea when he reminds us of what he calls the 'great inequity'. Disaster, whether natural or man-made, can destroy wealth and lives in enormous numbers with remarkable speed. Think of tsunamis or hedge fund collapses. But goodness requires millions of small actions accumulated over years and years to build happiness and prosperity. Please join me in this wonderful American tradition, and help to strengthen our nation for the future. You can do so by practicing the seven habits of generous people outlined in the final chapter of *Generosity Rules!*

CHAPTER 1

▼

DEFINING THE CYCLE OF GENEROSITY

Eugene Lang was the son of Hungarian immigrants living in New York City during the Great Depression. Like many children, he worked to help his family while going to school. His job was washing dishes in a restaurant. One evening, he was pressed into service as waiter. He was 14 years old.

He waited on a regular customer, who asked him about school. Gene said he wanted to go to college. The patron happened to be a trustee of Swarthmore College, a small private college in Pennsylvania. The man suggested that Gene might apply to Swarthmore, where there were scholarships available for able students. The year was 1935.

Fast forward to 1981. Gene Lang is back at PS 121 in Harlem to give a speech. The kids are mostly poor, and mostly the children of immigrants, just as they were when Gene was a student there. But now Gene is a very wealthy man, having used his talents and his Swarthmore education to launch numerous successful businesses. *Fortune Magazine* had called him 'the quintessential American entrepreneur' just a few years earlier.

The results of this encounter are now legendary in American philanthropic circles. On the spur of the moment, Lang promised each of the sixth graders two thousand dollars toward college tuition if they stayed in school and graduated. "I will keep my promise." he told them.

And, of course, he did, although he soon learned that putting the money on the table as an incentive was just the beginning of the help the kids required to succeed. But many ultimately did and Lang's generosity inspired dozens of other successful Americans to repeat his promise to inner city kids across America. The 'I Have a Dream' movement was born.

This story says it all about generosity in America. Citizen *generosity* is our secret weapon, our social and economic turbocharger, if you like. It generates *opportunities,* as the generosity of the Swarthmore trustee did for Gene Lang. And in the hands of a gifted individual like Lang, the opportunity led to *prosperity.* But the cycle did not stop with the prosperity of Lang, or his family, or even his many employees. Prosperity moved Lang to *gratitude;* for his own opportunities to succeed, and for the conditions beyond his control that had enabled his businesses to prosper. Inspired by this feeling, Lang renewed the cycle of generosity with his gift. In fact he expanded the cycle, by giving hundreds of gifts that greatly exceeded the single scholarship he had received many years earlier.

Generosity Rules! is inspired by the stories of Gene Lang and millions of other Americans who have fueled the cycle at the core of our national success. The history of American generosity is rich and complex, and it extends over three and one half centuries. But the core elements of the story do not change. Our economic and social progress is powered by a virtuous engine. The engine has four parts that work in a continuous, reinforcing cycle:

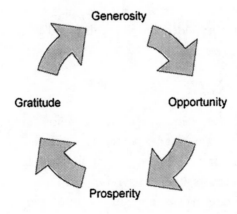

Generosity

Gratitude   Opportunity

Prosperity

GENEROSITY

Let's look at generosity to begin. Putting the greater good first in the new American colonies was essential. Settlers could not afford to ignore the well-being of any of their fellow colonists. Everyone was needed in the struggle, the well-born and the workers, the artisans and the book-educated. This was a Christian religious principle for the colonists, but it also made sense in order to insure one's own survival. "Self-interest, rightly understood", Alex de Tocqueville would call this distinctly American way of living.[2]

In 1630, this was a radical idea. The Massachusetts Bay settlers were determined to create an active Christian community in the new land. Each person would serve as 'his brother's keeper.' Inter-dependence launched many of the traditions we read about in grade school. Barn-raisings engaged the labor of the entire community to create homesteads for newly married couples. Community suppers, or 'pot lucks,' featured contributions from all families to a common meal. The settlers even developed the idea of a scholarship. They taxed themselves to pay for the education of (other peoples') able children, if their families were unable to pay the tuition. Over the next one hundred fifty years, inter-dependence evolved from a religious practice to a civic responsibility, and provided the launching pad for a new nation governed by 'we, the people'.

OPPORTUNITY

When Americans act generously toward fellow citizens, they create *opportunities*. Opportunities are powerful gifts when they enable people to pursue a dream or realize their potential. They develop 'human capital' as the economists like to say. Opportunities come in different forms as well. There may be a chance to re-develop a blighted neighborhood or a brownfield site. There may be a moment to apply a scientific insight to create a new medicine. We all benefit when these opportunities are exploited.

Happily, America is a genuine 'land of opportunity'. In countless acts of personal generosity, Americans have helped to enable justice for all through equal opportunities for poor people, minorities, newcomers and those with special needs. Our reputation for upward mobility as a society is well-earned over centuries.

Imagination and self-discipline are required to turn an opportunity into a success. We all know the clichés about opportunity only knocking once. But our tradition of generosity has given less privileged citizens a reason for initiative and optimism. Chapter III of *Generosity Rules!* is devoted to stories of opportunity created by generosity. For now, it is safe to say that without opportunities for many citizens, there is little chance of widespread prosperity.

PROSPERITY

We enjoy *prosperity* because of our social and economic mobility. While many opportunities have undoubtedly been wasted, many more have been exploited. Our very large 'middle class' lives at a higher level of income than in any other nation on earth. Given the ethnic and racial diversity of our population, this is a remarkable accomplishment. We also recognize that we have much more to do to create a truly just society, and this desire for progress carries us forward.

The willingness of private citizens to invest in equal opportunities for their fellow citizens powered the prosperity of the 'American Century'. We have nurtured the dreams of many more of our young people (and adults) than any other nation. We do so through a highly flexible educational system supported in large measure by private contributions (even many of the so-called 'public' universities receive the majority of their support from 'private' sources). Our investments have kept the

American dream alive for millions. These diverse individuals, in turn, have driven remarkable social and technical accomplishments in the twentieth and twenty-first centuries, from the light bulb to the personal computer, from the airplane to biotechnology, from integrated schools to greater access for the handicapped.

Prosperity is the focus of Chapter IV of *Generosity Rules!* We will consider the psychological, as well as the economic, prosperity we enjoy as a nation. We will also acknowledge the sacrifices made by so many citizens. Progress always has a price, and personal sacrifice will continue to be essential to our success.

GRATITUDE

Prosperity in America has had a very fortunate consequence. It has consistently generated *gratitude*. And gratitude, in turn, inspires generosity, enabling the cycle to begin all over again. A grateful person wants to 'give back' to a system that supported his or her success. Because Americans have a great tradition of giving across ethnic, racial, and religious boundaries, we are constantly seeding thankful individuals in all sectors of our democracy. We have created an epidemic of gratitude over hundreds of years, to the benefit of all society.

We were told as children that we should 'count our blessings.' We are learning that such behavior earns us more than points for cherubic behavior from our elders. Gratitude is one of the very best ways to maintain mental and physical health for ourselves. We will look at this fascinating research into instances of 'self-interest, rightly understood' in Chapter V. For now, I want to stress the linkage between the four elements of our American 'engine'. Generosity has contributed to opportunities for most of us to live without fear, to plan ahead, to borrow at reasonable rates, and to build a future. We have then been inspired to re-invest in America through our own generosity, recognizing that we have benefited from the gifts of others.

FUEL FOR THE ENGINE

Our generosity engine, like our market economy, runs on ideas. Both require a constant supply of new ideas to make better products, services and systems. We need the energy of moral and financial entrepreneurs to realize these possibilities. Everyone has ideas for improving the future, not simply the well-off. When we invest, we sustain optimism. Generous people ensure that everyone is able to bring their personal energy, drive, and imagination to the task of inventing a better future.

Young people are blessed with idealism, optimism, and energy, essential qualities for effective problem-solving. They are the reason to stress investments in education for the good of our nation. Our young people of every race and gender deserve access to the technologies that enable good ideas and lower the barriers to entry for budding entrepreneurs. Launching a business via the Web does not require the capital necessary to start a railroad or a newspaper. This deserves remembering when thinking about social capital building through education. It takes only a modest amount of help to produce genuine innovation from the fertile minds of (very) young entrepreneurs. Just ask Wendy Kopp, Sergey Brin or Ben Casnocha.[3]

These entrepreneurs sustain our 'American' commitment to improvement, to improving our homes, to improving ourselves, and to improving the lot of others who are less fortunate than we are. Citizen generosity is essential to sustaining our progress. We have "a little engine that could" in our cycle of helping one another. This cycle has powered America's social and economic progress for three hundred fifty years. I firmly believe it must remain an inspiration for us all going forward.

CHAPTER 2

▼

GENEROSITY

Personal generosity begins and ends the cycle that empowers our nation. Generosity initiates a cascade of outcomes that benefit individuals and, ultimately, the nation as a whole. I believe that American generosity is rooted in our sense of a shared future with our fellow citizens. We are all neighbors. We insist on justice for all because that 'all' includes us. Our generosity originates in our embrace of 'self-interest, rightly understood'.

What exactly constitutes personal generosity? For many of us raised in the faiths of Abraham, which encompass Judaism, Islam, and Christianity, the story of 'the good Samaritan' exemplifies generosity. Jesus was quizzed by some learned men about the meaning of his injunction to 'love thy neighbor as thyself'. Who, they asked, was Jesus referring to when he used the word 'neighbor'? In response, Jesus recounted the tale of a Jew who had been mugged, robbed, and abandoned by the roadside. While several observant religious travelers passed him by, a stranger from Samaria stopped to offer assistance. This generous man carried the victim to a nearby inn, paid the bill, and instructed the innkeeper to care for the man as needed. He assured the keeper that he would pay any additional bills when he passed back along the road on his way home.

Jesus asked his questioners which traveler had acted as a neighbor. The point was clear. One's neighbor is any other person, no matter the surface differences of race, ethnicity, class, religion or geography. By caring for another in the same manner we would wish to be cared for ourselves, we build a stronger human community.

We should all know the story of the Good Samaritan by heart, regardless of our religious beliefs or heritage. It's a memorable tale of taking personal responsibility despite the availability of many excuses to do otherwise. The story introduces the theme of charity (the Greek root of which is the word for love). Charity is the first component of generosity. It defines our responsibility to meet the basic needs of all humans, especially the victims of poverty, violence or natural disaster.

Happily, this impulse to charity is alive and well in America. Whenever fellow citizens face a disaster that leaves people in need of shelter, food, and clothing, Americans respond. We do so without regard to the race, ethnicity, or location of the victims. We are driven by compassion and by gratitude for our good fortune to have been spared. We respond instinctively to those less fortunate than we are, and this is as it should be.

American generosity, however, has an additional component. 'Philanthropy' refers to generosity that goes beyond meeting a basic human need. Philanthropy seeks a longer term improvement in the well-being of an individual or a group. It provides an investment of time and/or money that is expected to acquire value in the future. The term 'philanthropy' is also based on a Greek word that means 'love', but I like to use it for our distinctive American form of investment generosity. It reminds me of Philadelphia, the city of 'brotherly love' where our Declaration of Independence was drafted.

American philanthropists are investors. We invest in people through training and education. We invest in physical assets: museums, hospitals, university laboratories, parks, and churches. We also invest in ideas: medical research, legal reforms, and new technologies. These investments are seldom 'spontaneous' as a charitable gift might be. They are more often the result of our own thinking about a social problem or our response to a reasoned appeal from an organization or individual.

American philanthropy is driven by our sense of justice. Gottfried Leibniz, an influential 18th century German mathematician/philosopher, called justice the 'soul of generosity.' It is 'just' that all citizens have an opportunity to develop their gifts through education, not only those born into families with the ability to pay the bills. It is 'just' that every citizen enjoy access to beautiful art or great theater, not only those who can afford to buy great paintings or to sponsor private performances. We demand justice for ourselves. We must therefore demand justice for others as well and act on this expectation. We are, after all, doing no more than loving our neighbor as we love ourselves.

The best news is how well this works out for all concerned. We have inherited a wonderful legacy from the colonists who founded our nation. John Winthrop, the eventual governor of the Massachusetts Bay colony, laid out his vision in a memorable sermon just before his ship arrived on shore in 1630.

> "In this new land, he wrote, we must be knit together in this worke as one man, we must entertaine eachother in brotherly Affeccion, we must be willing to abridge ourselves of our superfluities, for the supply of others' necessities...." [4]

Winthrop was determined to put this vision into action in a great social experiment. He believed in the counter-intuitive Biblical wisdom about generosity in Proverbs 11:

> One man gives freely, yet gains even more. Another withholds unduly, but comes to poverty. A generous man will prosper.

Every life was to be nurtured, despite differences in wealth, skills and abilities. Everyone was to be accountable to everyone else, rather than to the King or to God alone. Moreover, and here we find the first connection to capitalism, the settlers were all members of a corporation. They were chartered as a fur trading company, and funds for their trip had been raised by selling shares, with some wealthy colonists owning many shares and others owning only a few. In some cases, the well-to-do had purchased shares for the benefit of the smithies, bakers, and hunters who made up an important part of the company. Company members were thus held together economically, socially, and spiritually. Survival depended on the pooling of everyone's time, treasure and talents. Inter-dependence and mutuality were the starting point for this first corporation and later for the nation as a whole.

If the answer to 'why be generous?' is 'because this is how to survive and prosper', the logical follow-up question is: 'How, exactly, should we put generosity into action?' A very thoughtful answer is provided by another hero of the 'faiths of Abraham', the rabbi Maimonides. In the 12th century, he offered an elaborate analysis of how to give in the chapter of his codebook dedicated to agriculture. He laid out eight stages of alms-giving, beginning with those who see giving as an opportunity to draw attention to their own superiority. Such givers are not afraid to publicize their own generosity, no matter how modest, or to dismiss those in need as inferior. But, as Maimonides points out, at least they are giving something.

You might imagine that the eighth stage involves a giver who is as generous as possible as frequently as possible, who gives anonymously, and who respects the dignity of the recipient. But this behavior constitutes only the seventh stage in his hierarchy of generosity. The final and most admirable stage is partnership with the recipient. The eighth stage celebrates the value of all humans just as John Winthrop preached several hundred years later in Massachusetts.

Maimonides established a vision of how to give that endures today, one in which all acts of generosity are worthy of admiration, no matter how flawed. Generosity is ultimately about recognizing ourselves in the 'other'. It acknowledges that we are indeed 'all in it together'. We cannot afford to waste the gifts of any citizen, no matter how modest they may be.

Generosity proves to be the beginning and the end of our cycle of growth in America. As we look ahead, we can see that providing opportunities to fellow citizens through generosity has fueled an engine of prosperity for millions of Americans, whether newcomers or longtime residents. This has not happened overnight. There have been centuries of racism and sexism in 'the newe land'. But we have maintained our optimism and our commitments. We have struggled to achieve the Founding Fathers idealized commitment to life, liberty and the pursuit of happiness. Generosity should be celebrated for keeping this dream alive.

▼

CHAPTER 3

OPPORTUNITY

Opportunity is the second element of the virtuous cycle. It is created for us by citizen generosity. This simple fact is a cornerstone of our political and economic success. Americans value opportunity. Opportunities bring together our optimism and our entrepreneurial, action orientation. Citizens who invest in the creation of opportunities for others deserve our admiration because they often take great risks in pursuit of a 'level playing field'. They have understood that 'equal opportunity' for all citizens is essential to the greater good of which they are themselves a part.

Osceola McCarty is another legend of American philanthropy. She was a sharecropper's daughter who made her living as a laundress. In 1995, she gave $150,000 to the University of Southern Mississippi. Her reasoning for making the gift was as straightforward as her lifelong saving strategy:

> They used not to let colored people go out there, but now they do, and I think they should have it. I just want the scholarship to go to some child who needs it. I'm too old (she was 87 at the time) to get an education, but they can.[5]

Our American appreciation of opportunity is deeply ingrained. We prefer to see luck as 'preparation meeting opportunity', rather than some capricious intervention of divine forces. This view reflects the kind of faith in the future that Osceola McCarty demonstrated. If you believe that life just 'happens' and that you are simply a pawn in the greater scheme of things, then the idea of an opportunity is meaningless. On the other hand, when you believe that the future can be different from the present and that you have the power to change it, then you value opportunity.

Opportunity is a moment to be 'seized', something to prepare for because it 'only knocks once'. It is precious and not to be 'wasted'. We assess opportunity 'cost' when we recognize that something valuable, another opportunity, has been set aside when we choose option A over option B.

The Founding Fathers valued opportunity as the most basic of rights. In the Declaration of Independence, they wrote of the "right to life, liberty and the pursuit of happiness." Not a right to happiness, but to the opportunity to pursue it. The writers were well aware that these rights were not enjoyed by everyone in the new nation. But they aspired to create a nation where such a vision could be pursued. These rights, they reminded the colonists, could not be assured by the government. They could not be assured by 'the church.' They could only be assured by 'we, the people' acting in our capacity as free, private citizens. It is up to each of us to make certain that others enjoy these opportunities. In so doing, we ensure that they will work on our behalf. As the signers of the Declaration of Independence noted in closing, we pledge to each other "our lives, our fortunes, and our sacred honor."

We still value opportunity just as highly today because it represents a chance for a better future. We embrace the right to follow our dreams in earning a living, or owning a house, or starting a business. And we still enjoy a national consensus in favor of a 'level playing field' (given our love of sports metaphors). We believe that justice requires every player to have an equal opportunity to compete, and to rise to the best level of his or her God-given ability. Martin Luther King did not dream of success for all black Americans in his famous 'I have a dream' speech. He dreamed simply the American dream, that everyone would have an equal chance to pursue their opportunities. Speaking of the rights promised in the Declaration of Independence, King argued that the Negro had received a 'bad check' from our nation rather than a valuable promissory note. He concluded his metaphor as follows:

> We refuse to believe that there are insufficient funds in the great vaults of opportunity of this nation.[6]

Today, we enjoy many more laws to prevent discrimination and to level the playing field. But the pathway to opportunity always begins with generosity. A scholarship for a needy student creates opportunity through generosity. Ensuring that a capable student can pursue education as far as his or her abilities allow is an investment with many benefits, including the vote of confidence in the future of another person. Such confidence, in turn, bolsters that person's self-confidence and will to succeed. Our nation is filled with millions of such benefactors, starting with Anne Radcliffe who gave the first scholarship to Harvard in

1643. Since those days private citizens have donated billions and billions of dollars to fund the education of capable students.

I'm certain that you know a great example of such an investment yourself. I often think when I visit a hospital or a school that the doctors, nurses and teachers should wear nametags with more than their names. The tags should also say 'Brought to you by ...' followed by the name of the donor(s) who provided the scholarships that enabled these individuals to complete their training. I bet there would be many such tags. Just try to imagine, for a moment, what your town would look like if all those citizens who went to college on private scholarships were no longer in their positions of responsibility.

Generosity produces opportunities for more than education, of course. I am always moved by the story of the Mothers March of Dimes, a veritable army of believers who collected four billion dimes to fuel an opportunity. In this case, it was the chance to exploit the emerging knowledge of vaccines to prevent polio. They seized the moment and persevered for seventeen years to ensure that this opportunity was not wasted.

George Peabody created another kind of equal opportunity for his fellow citizens. Before the end of the Civil War, Peabody underwrote the construction of several public facilities in Baltimore, Maryland, including a museum, a gallery, and a music school. He later created natural history museums in New Haven, Connecticut, and Cambridge, Massachusetts. His commitment to bring art, music and science to all citizens inspired several generations of wealthy Americans, the Morgans, Fricks, and Guggenheims among them, to also invest in such facilities. Most of our public libraries, theaters, parks, museums, and concert halls across the nation came into being in just this way. Each such facility provides an equal opportunity for all citizens to enjoy our greatest treasures.

These citizens acted on their beliefs. Without action, opportunity means nothing. Taking action, of course, also involves taking risk. There is always the possibility of failure whenever opportunity is pursued. In many cultures, failure, particularly the failure of an enterprise, carries great stigma. It is hardly surprising that entrepreneurs are few and far between in such settings. I love the idea that our nation has been built by a combination of 'financial' entrepreneurs, those seeking to build great fortunes, and 'moral' entrepreneurs, those bringing the same drive, passion, and resourcefulness to amassing 'social' profit that enriches the greater good.

Generosity that enables action when an opportunity arises provides a great advantage in America. The two per cent of GDP that Americans, individually and through foundations, contribute to the social profit sector year after year has created a venture pool for investment in high risk opportunities. Decades ago, a Scotsman named Alexander Fleming showed up in America seeking support for a 'long shot' idea. He wanted to turn the mold on his Petrie dish into medicine to fight infections. He had been unable to find support in Europe from either private investors or governments. He did find an American philanthropist willing to support his work, not for monetary gain, but because the investor saw an opportunity and was willing to take a very high risk. The result of Rockefeller's bias in favor of risk-taking resulted in Fleming's discovery of penicillin.

We are all beneficiaries of this American bias for action. We say "nothing ventured, nothing gained." We are prepared to fail. When givers become so conservative that they fund only 'sure bets', we become impatient. There has been a backlash against our wealthiest universities and their multi-billion dollar endowments in recent years. Although these dollars have been donated by generous friends and alumni, Americans have the nerve to ask how creatively the accumulated funds are being used. Why not release all scholarship students from loans? Why not fund some school teachers to study at the great university? Only in America do we expect more of our social profit leaders: more risk-taking, more innovation, and more breakthroughs with our philanthropic investments.

Today 'venture' philanthropy is in vogue. Successful business entrepreneurs are seeking to apply their skills, experience, and imagination to solving social problems at the local, and in some cases, global level. We are fortunate that our traditions of citizen generosity are alive and well among these skilled, experienced people. The social profit sector needs all the talented leaders it can find. But 'venture philanthropy,' to my mind, is simply the continuation of the search for opportunity that has characterized high-risk social investment throughout our nation's history.

What could be more venture-driven than the efforts of Jane Addams, our first female Nobel Prize recipient? As our nation's economy was transformed from agriculture to manufacturing during the late 19th century, northern American cities were flooded by job seekers from overseas and from the rural South. Poverty and disease were rampant in the crowded tenements of Pittsburgh, Chicago, Detroit, and New York. Addams, a well-to-do, college-educated woman with no particular experience in solving social problems, recruited other educated women to visit the tenements and ultimately to live for periods of time among the poor. Her goal was to understand better the challenges they faced. This field research, funded by Addams and other donors, led her to create 'settlement houses' in the poor communities.

These community centers provided job training, language training, urban living skills, parenting skills, even music lessons, through a network of volunteers in dozens of cities across America. These risky efforts paid off. They produced the work force that enabled America to prosper in the emerging age of steel, railroads and automobiles. They also produced many of the musicians who populated America's first symphony orchestras.

I cannot think of a higher risk investment than backing a group of young, inexperienced, book-educated women to solve work force preparedness issues for a nation in transition. Yet Addams and her colleagues did exactly that. They committed to ensuring opportunities for all, for newcomers from overseas, for blacks and poor whites from the war-torn South, for women and children as well as men. Their thoughtful, well-organized initiative drove one of our great national success stories.

Opportunity is about freedom, freedom from a pre-destined future because of one's gender, race, or economic circumstance. It is about freedom to visit a new place, to explore a new idea, or to invent a new way of doing something. This freedom is at the core of American creativity. It has been brought to us by generous citizens looking out for opportunities for others. Without opportunities, there can be no prosperity. But with opportunities for so many citizens, the result has been unprecedented prosperity for our nation.

CHAPTER 4

▼

PROSPERITY

Prosperity is the third element of the cycle of generosity. Prosperity has two requirements. We must have the proper conditions for prosperity, in the form of equal opportunities and equal access for all citizens. We can call these conditions 'justice for all.' Secondly, we must have the personal self-discipline and energy to do something with our opportunities. We have a strong tradition of striving to 'do' justice in America. We also expect individual citizens to take personal responsibility when conditions are 'just'. I believe citizen generosity has driven both components of prosperity.

We think of prosperity in financial terms in our information intensive world. Most of us keep a mental 'scorecard' to track how we are doing. Did I make more this year than last? How much is my house worth? How much do I have in my retirement account this month? All that scorekeeping data is just a couple of mouse clicks away.

The government also contributes to scorekeeping with an avalanche of data every month. We measure how we are doing in creating new jobs, reducing unemployment, increasing the GDP, and how many new pickup trucks we are buying. This data is available to policy makers, to financial professionals, and to everyone else, instantaneously.

Such documented progress is all very new. Before the Industrial Revolution of the 19th century, the possibility of human "progress" was highly debated. But we now have come to expect that each generation will be better off than the previous one, and with good reason. By most economic measures, we are much better off than we were even a short while ago. The average work week is now thirty five hours. In 1900, it was sixty hours. Today ninety percent of manufacturing workers take a vacation. One hundred years ago only six percent did.[7]

There are additional quantitative measures of our prosperity as well. If you translate the annual income of an average citizen in 1929 into today's dollars, the result is about $16,000.[8] In other words, the entire middle class was 'poor' by modern standards. In the 1960's, when Lyndon Johnson declared a 'war on poverty', there were millions of rural poor living without electricity, running water, or schools. The poor are still with us. The same proportion of our citizens (about thirteen percent) lives below the official poverty level as did so in the '60's. Today, however, these folks do have the above-mentioned amenities, no matter how unpleasant their living conditions may be. They also continue to do better, despite a very disturbing increase in income disparity between rich and poor. The earnings of the lowest twenty percent of wage earners increased by about eighty percent over the past fifteen years, while earnings for those in the middle class increased by only twenty percent.[9]

Using these economic yardsticks, we have achieved a remarkable level of prosperity and done so very quickly. These accomplishments are the result of investments we have made, as generous individuals and as a nation. Generous citizens have often led the way in making far-sighted, high risk commitments when 'prosperity' was far from certain at the time of their investments. The most obvious investments have been those in our 'human capital'. The early opportunities for broad access to education in our nation, driven by philanthropists, have been leveraged to great advantage. Our workforce, despite persistent shortcomings in our public education system, is among the best educated in the world. Ready or not, globalization is here to stay, and globalization has increased the economic value of education. The more education one has achieved, the greater the income that can be earned. It is as simple as that.

According to the U.S. Census Bureau, workers without any kind of school diploma averaged about $19,000 in annual wages in 2004. By contrast, holders of a bachelor's degree averaged over $51,000 per year and those with advanced degrees over $78,000. It is difficult to think of a better, higher yielding 'investment' than supporting the education of a fellow citizen.[10]

It is remarkable to me that the early colonists grasped the importance of educating all citizens (at least all white men) to the highest level of their ability. I've already mentioned Anne Radcliffe, who gave a scholarship to educate someone else's son over three hundred fifty years ago. When we talk about gratitude in the next chapter, we will meet a few more of the millions of scholarship donors who, in gratitude for their own good fortune, have chosen to give back to the greater good through scholarships.

Julius Rosenwald is the most impressive private investor in education I have met in my research. He was not a scholarship donor. He was a builder, an investor in the physical capital needed to run an educational enterprise. Rosenwald was the son of poor, Jewish immigrants from Germany. As a teenager in the 1880's, he got a job as a stock boy for a new merchandising company based in Chicago. Some time later, he proposed to his bosses that it would make sense to create a booklet with pictures of the merchandise, so that customers could pick out what they wanted and have it delivered (perhaps Julius thought that he would no longer have to carry the stuff up to the showroom floor for the customers to examine!) In any case, Julius later became the CEO of Sears Roebuck, America's largest retailer. His Sears catalogue became part of life for millions of Americans.

While running Sears, he embarked on a trip around the country, only to discover that in the post-Civil War South, eighty percent of black children were not in school. In fact, they didn't even have schools to attend. Rosenwald knew that this situation could not be good for the country, or for his business. He crafted a plan in partnership with Booker T. Washington, the champion of education for blacks who had founded Tuskegee Institute in Alabama. Rosenwald proposed that he would match, with his own money, the funds raised toward school construction by any of the communities that lacked schools.

It's a long story, but over the years, Rosenwald helped to build 5,327 schools, some of which are still in operation. He personally invested over four million dollars, a sum worth many times that amount today. More importantly, his partnering approach brought equal donations from the black community, additional funds from foundations, and finally a commitment from the federal government.

There is much more to tell about Julius Rosenwald. He supported the construction of YMCA's (remember, he was a Jew) in dozens of cities because he saw the value of community centers. He also funded the nation's first Museum of Science and Industry in Chicago that continues to draw visitors today. But let's focus on his support to education. His leadership, personal generosity and risk taking are simply exemplary. Well before our government grasped the importance of investing in universal public education, or college loans and scholarships, he created opportunities for fellow citizens that paved the way for the industrial successes of the 20th century.

Prosperity is a psychological, as well as an economic, condition. The very fact that an individual is enabled to affect his or her own future has enormous positive consequences. There has been an explosion of research in 'positive' psychology in recent years, and much of it is really about prosperity. Rather than exploring only mental illnesses and deviant behaviors, the field has sought to understand what makes people happy and optimistic. In short, what are the factors that enable people to thrive?

Our drive to acquire wealth and status offers a typical problem. The majority of people who progress on the economic ladder, often through very hard work and sacrifice, report that they are not any 'happier' as a result of this accomplishment. So why do they continue this kind of behavior? Current thinking will not surprise you. There is greater pleasure to be derived from the pursuit of a goal than from its attainment. It is the journey, not the destination, which provides the positive experience and feeling of empowerment.[11]

Another problem to consider: prosperity does not create animosity between income groups in America. Why do researchers find little resentment of the rich among 'poor' people, given that the income gap between these two groups has been growing rapidly over the past two decades? This is not, by the way, the case in most European countries where, despite a much smaller income gap, there is considerable anger and resentment among the poor. *The New York Times* reported recently on efforts to unionize the gardeners and janitors who work on Fisher Island, an exclusive enclave just off Miami. It is difficult to find a more extreme case of income disparity. The laborers earn less than ten dollars per hour while the average net worth of the two thousand inhabitants exceeds ten million dollars each. Although this is a single case, the results of the union's research parallel the findings of a much larger, complex study of 'happiness'. The laborers do wish for greater income to support their families, but are unwilling to find fault with the island dwellers because of their great wealth.[12]

The workers were not responding this way because they feared losing their jobs. These workers, like generations before them, can envision prosperity in America, whether for themselves or for their children. It is this process of anticipation, just as middle class workers anticipate the pleasures of owning a time share or a nicer car, that provides a measurable sense of satisfaction and optimism. Personal effort and sacrifice have a purpose. Progress is not just possible, but within the control of the individual.

There is also new scientific research that seeks to document the impact of generosity, not on the recipient, but on the donor. While much of this work is in its early stages, there is plenty of encouraging information. Stephen Post[13] has collected data from a variety of researchers studying the effects of 'altruism' on mental and physical health. All signs point to benefits for the giver. Most of us can think of our own examples of this phenomenon, whether we have definitive 'scientific' studies or not. Just ask a local volunteer for Habitat for Humanity, or for a school reading program who gets the most out of their efforts. I think of my mother-in-law, still going strong at ninety six in the modest, suburban home she built over sixty years, still caring for the ever-changing cast of young neighbors on her block with baked goods and childrearing advice, while being cared for in return on a daily basis. This is American prosperity of the highest order.

The virtuous cycle thus completes itself with the givers as well as the recipients. By ensuring the possibility of prosperity for another person, one takes the best care of oneself and one's own possibilities. This strategy ultimately achieves the partnership between donor and recipient that Julius Rosenwald pursued. The Founding Fathers called the pursuit of happiness an inalienable right, up there with life and liberty. As guarantors of each other's rights, we all have the responsibility to provide this opportunity to each other.

The Founding Fathers were certainly idealistic when they crafted our Declaration of Independence. Given a set of colonies filled with slaves, violence, and prejudice, they needed great vision to imagine how things should work in the new republic. But they did have examples of the power of mutuality in the Massachusetts Bay colony. I believe that the Declaration of Independence was made possible by the Declaration of 'Inter-dependence' articulated by John Winthrop some one hundred fifty years earlier.

Julius Rosenwald kept this idealism alive over one hundred years later. He was motivated by his business interests. He wanted his business and his employees to thrive. But he also understood that this could not happen in the face of such an obvious injustice as a lack of schools for some children He committed himself to justice first, taking a bold risk that this was the best way to prosperity. Rosenwald also insisted on a partnership with those in need. In so doing, he engaged those he helped in taking action on their own behalf. He offered psychological prosperity.

I will never forget the woman I met when giving a speech in New Orleans a few years back. When I finished telling a story about Rosenwald's generosity, she rose from the audience with tears in her eyes. She exclaimed to her assembled colleagues, a crowd of several hundreds representing social profit organizations throughout Louisiana, that *she* was a graduate of a Rosenwald School. Soon several of her colleagues were on their feet as well, witnessing to their own Rosenwald experiences. These successful, powerful, prosperous women, recipients of generosity offered over one hundred years ago, are today giving back to the community that gave them an opportunity to succeed.

As we shall see in the next chapter, we as a nation are rewarded with gratitude on all sides for such an environment, and gratitude is our surest launching pad for sustained generosity.

CHAPTER 5

▼

GRATITUDE

Gratitude is the fourth component of the virtuous cycle. Prosperity builds our sense of gratitude as we recognize that we are each beneficiaries of the generosity of others. In America, we even express our thankfulness with a national holiday, Thanksgiving Day. Our gratitude motivates us to offer a 'hand up' to fellow citizens striving for participation in prosperity. Such actions lay the groundwork for the virtuous cycle of generosity to begin all over again.

When I was a scholarship student in the 1960's, the dean of students at Connecticut College saw to it that I sent a hand-written thank you note to my benefactors each year. This was not a casual responsibility, but a formal obligation, right up there with signing the honor pledge on each assignment I submitted. I'm pretty certain that I would have done the right thing even without the heavy hand of Dean Noyes on my shoulder, but the institution made certain that each scholarship student acknowledged, by name and in our own handwriting, the gifts that enabled us to enjoy a Conn College education. My husband was a 'mid-western scholarship boy' at Princeton during the same period and he was required to do the same thing. Today we are even more grateful for our scholarships than we were in our callow teenage years.

As president of my alma mater years later, I hosted an annual luncheon that brought together scholarship recipients with the donors of their scholarships. These events were always fascinating, if sometimes fraught with a bit of tension on all sides. No one knew quite what to expect (including me)!

I particularly remember introducing Saja Mohammed to her benefactors. Saja had been the valedictorian of Bridgeport, CT High School. She was black, Muslim, and already an outspoken member of the campus community as a freshman. The first member of her family to attend college, she was planning to become a doctor. Her scholarship covered room, board, tuition, books, travel to and from Bridgeport, medical expenses (including her first visit to a dentist), a clothing allowance, and a living allowance (I later discovered that she was sending the allowance home, a reminder that I had sold my gym suit freshman year to pay for textbooks). The donors were represented by three generations of Connecticut College alumnae, a recent grad, her mother, and her grandmother, an elegant Boston matron from the class of '37.

When it was Saja's turn to say a few words, she rose from her place and embraced the slightly startled grandmother warmly. She declared that her first priority upon graduating was to earn enough money that she, too, could give a scholarship to Connecticut College, or as she put it, "to send the elevator back down for someone else, just like you sent the elevator for me."

This moment has defined American gratitude for me ever since. Of course we ought to write thank you notes. It is a basic social grace, a fundamental of the civility toward one another that we rely on to lubricate the flow of daily life. But the American way of gratitude includes more than rituals of acknowledgment. It is accompanied by action. In Saja's case, and in millions of others like hers (including my own), the beneficiaries express gratitude through gifts of their own time and money. When Anne Radcliffe gave that first scholarship to Harvard back in 1643, the farmers whose sons benefited from her generosity started their own 'fund' within a decade, donating corn and other foodstuffs to Harvard. The endowments at many American colleges, both public and private, have been built by generations of scholarship recipients giving back to enable the next generation of worthy students to find support. Most hospitals likewise receive significant support, in dollars and in volunteered services, from thankful patients and their families.

This mindset of action/gratitude is a clear economic asset to our nation. When we focus on what others have done to help us, we activate our own 'inner entrepreneur'. We do not want to disappoint those who have given us a chance, and we act with energy to prove that they have made a wise investment

The results are frequently impressive. Bill Clinton and Oprah were scholarship students at college, as were Ruth Ginsburg, Richard Nixon, and Mark Rothko to pick some names at random. All have used their prestige and influence to offer a 'hand-up' to those in need. Following the advice of Andrew Carnegie to give back to society, Bill Gates, Ted Turner, Warren Buffett, Michael Bloomberg, Eli Broad and dozens of additional 21st century philanthropists have all offered a version of this rationale as they have contributed their accumulated personal wealth to improving the nation and the world.

While the rich and famous attract the attention of the media, gratitude works powerfully at the grass roots level as well. Remember, eighty nine percent of Americans made a contribution last year, and people in the lowest forty percent of the income distribution gave more, as a percentage of their incomes, than did the wealthiest Americans. We are blessed with tens of millions of contributors each year to our churches, synagogues and mosques that together provide billions of dollars worth of social services to their communities. Millions more contribute to local United Way campaigns, community foundations, and giving circles. And millions more contribute their time to Habitat for Humanity, the Boys and Girls Clubs, the Scouts, and countless local causes.

Our greatest strength as a nation comes from this 'grass-roots' gratitude, because gratitude drives our optimism. Wise people have intuited the psychological benefits of gratitude throughout the ages, and those religions that have advised daily prayers of thanksgiving, it turns out, have anticipated the benefits being documented scientifically today. Gratitude has become a lively topic of study among psychologists, following the same drive to understand the bases of psychological good health that has increased research into generosity and happiness.

In a recent study, participants who kept a daily record of thoughts and occurrences for which they were 'thankful' derived benefits in many desirable categories: alertness, optimism, enthusiasm, determination, and energy, compared to those who did not track these feelings, or those who recorded only unhappy events.[14]

When we focus on the good things in our lives, we have reason to celebrate, and a reason to take action on behalf of others. This is good for us as individuals, and even better for our nation as a whole. America's economic engine runs on an ever-increasing supply of gratitude. It is not a coincidence that our nation is the only one with a national holiday to celebrate 'thanksgiving'. American is home to the Center for World Thanksgiving.[15] Our most American of national holidays is a day of gratitude.

By remembering all that we have to be thankful for, all the opportunities we have enjoyed in our nation, we position ourselves to 'do the right thing', to recycle our privilege to those in need, to reinvest in opportunities for others. Through gratitude, we give birth to the next cycle of generosity.

▼

CHAPTER 6

SEVEN HABITS OF HIGHLY GENEROUS PEOPLE

(with apologies to Steven Covey)

1. Count Your Sheep (err, Blessings) Every Day

2. Never Ask Your Doctor Whether Generosity is Right for You

3. Lead With Your Heart but Follow Your Head

4. Liberate Your Inner Hedge Fund Manager

5. Be Like Nelson (Mandela): Each One Teach One

6. Leave a Legacy to Your Family

7. Put on Your Cheerleader Outfit

I hope that you have been inspired by our tradition of American generosity to think about your own giving. If so, I'd like to offer a list of 'habits' for you to consider, with apologies to Steven Covey. Covey is the author of *The Seven Habits of Highly Effective People*, the classic American guide to self-improvement that has sold tens of millions of copies.

Habits are practices for daily living and generosity is very much a way of living every day. Here are some habits that have helped me. I hope that they provide you with food for thought on your own journey to contribute to the greater good.

1. Count Your Sheep (err, Blessings) Every Day

I think that 'making gratitude your attitude' is the single most important thing you can do to practice generosity. We are all beneficiaries of the generosity of our fellow citizens. We owe our security and comfort to a combination of hard work, the good lord, and our fellow citizens. If we keep our own good fortune in focus on a daily basis, we are much more likely to remember the needs of others.

2. Never Ask Your Doctor Whether Generosity is Right for You

Generosity is right for everyone. It is completely guilt-free. Do not feel overwhelmed or put off by the attention that the media give to the mega-givers. Every gift, like every vote, does count. Warren Buffet gave thirty one billion dollars in 2006. In fact twenty one Americans each gave one hundred million or more. That is pretty intimidating. But remember, Buffet's gift constituted only about two percent of 2006 individual charitable giving.

We should applaud these remarkable gifts and get right back to thinking about how we can each make a difference through giving that matches the scale of our capacity. If you are ever made to feel that the size of your gift is all that matters, find another social profit organization to support. Generosity is never about the size of a gift.

3. Lead With Your Heart, but Follow Your Head.

Go ahead. Lead with your heart. Give spontaneously when there is a local appeal to help the victims of a house fire, or a family overwhelmed by medical expenses because of a sick child. You don't have to worry about whether it is a good investment or whether your contribution will be used wisely. Who cares what a homeless person does with a few dollars when one look at him (or her) tells you the person is clearly needy?

But generosity is more than charity. Bring your head with you as well as your heart when you invest through social profit organizations. Don't be afraid to ask how exactly your contribution will be deployed. It is not impolite to inquire. What percentage of your donation will go directly to support single mothers or abandoned pets?

Volunteering your time to join the board of a social profit organization will enable you to understand how the organization really works and how effective the leadership is. You certainly consider yourself a good thinker in your daily life. You sort the good from the not-so-good and you push yourself and others to optimize the use of resources. Do the same for your generosity.

4. Liberate Your Inner Hedge Fund Manager

It is prudent to invest wisely. All investments carry risk. But don't make the mistake of applying the same calculus to your social investments that you apply to your personal savings.

Social investing needs to be high risk. You are betting, in many cases, on 'turn-around' situations where the odds of success are very long. Changing destructive human behavior or deeply ingrained prejudices will never be a 'sure thing.' We need 'shots on goal' for difficult problems, with the hope that sooner or later we will find a solution that can be broadly adopted. Consider giving to a few 'crazy' ideas that could make a great difference if they were successful.

I recommend an experimental approach to your generosity, if you find yourself to be uncertain in the face of many demands. There are no right or wrong decisions in these matters. Consider focusing your generosity on a local problem for a fixed period of time, and let your 'neighbors' know that your commitment is limited. Learn all you can through the experience and, if you are still drawn to other needs, move on. Devote your time and treasure to a new cause, perhaps one that is very different from the original choice. The personal rewards of this approach are great.

5. Each One Teach One

Do as Nelson Mandela urged his fellow prisoners to do while he was jailed in South Africa. Teach at least one other person what you know. The best way to teach generosity is to learn some of the stories that are recounted here or in *The Greater Good*.

- Want to illustrate that it's not always about rich people giving the big bucks? Tell people the story of the Mother's March of Dimes to find a cure for polio.

- Have an opportunity to demonstrate that many great ideas came from philanthropists before the government caught on? Point to Anne Radcliffe giving the first scholarship to the son of a working class guy in 1643 (the government didn't offer support for scholarships until after World War II).

- Have a well-to-do friend who doesn't really think he ever got help from a philanthropist? Tell him (or her) the story of Alfred Cowles who funded the creation of econometrics and modern portfolio theory with his own money through the Cowles Institute. (Institute fellows have been awarded nine Nobel Prizes in economics over the years).

You should also learn the stories that make up the philanthropic history of your local community or region. Your goal is to increase the philanthropic literacy of your friends and colleagues. Everyone needs to understand the basics of how our market economy, representative democracy, and citizen commitment to generosity have built our nation. I think there is special importance to this task as we have so many 'newcomers' to America. You have an important role to play in telling our story.

6. Leave a Legacy to Your Family

Whatever else you do, help the younger members of your family to explore the idea of 'we, the people'. Our nation needs a new generation of 'civic superheroes' to ensure a just and prosperous future for all citizens. There should be regular family conversations (perhaps each Thanksgiving?) about plans for giving both time and money. Children can research programs and organizations that interest them, and report back to the family. Over time, more complicated questions about levels of generosity and risk can be addressed. I can assure you that your children or grandchildren will learn important lessons about personal responsibility through these kinds of conversations about thoughtful generosity.

I also recommend viewing the 2005 film, *Batman Begins*. The hero, young Bruce Wayne, is not a superhuman creature from another planet. He is a child of privilege. He learns about generosity from his parents, who explain their civic-mindedness in simple terms: 'Gotham has been good to us.' Eventually Bruce overcomes many challenges, including his own personal fears, to save the citizens of his community from selfish, vengeful enemies. Consider renting the DVD some evening and viewing this superhero story in the light of citizen generosity. I think you will find it intelligent and challenging for a family discussion. (WARNING: the film has violence and very scary special effects that, at least to me, would not be appropriate for kids below their teens.)

I think all kids are idealists to begin with and they enjoy an instinctive sense of what is just, whether on the ball field or in the classroom. We must take responsibility to nurture these wonderful assets, fight cynicism, and convey to them a legacy of citizen responsibility, no matter how wealthy (or not so wealthy) your family may be.

7. Put on Your Cheerleader Outfit

We all know how difficult it is to get media attention for a 'good news' story. "If it bleeds, it leads" as they say in the newspaper business. Generous people should want to share the good news about our secret weapon. They should want to celebrate generosity, on Thanksgiving Day, and on other days as well.

The best place to start is your own home town. The best way to start is an event that involves as many local citizens as possible. A dinner for United Way major donors? The annual meeting of the community foundation board? Such events are important building blocks, but they have limited impact. Why not more clean up days at local parks or food drives with multiple collection points? Each makes for great 'photo ops' for the local paper.

I've been fortunate to participate in many local celebrations of generosity. I remember the wonderful work of the Selby Foundation in Sarasota, FL. During 'Philanthropy Week', they enabled every citizen in town to be a 'philanthropist for a day' by promising to donate fifty dollars to a local social profit organization in the name of any local citizen who asked.

There is no shortage of good ideas for how to celebrate, but celebrate we must. This is one tradition in America that deserves a celebration which equals the Fourth of July. Freedom is a wonderful value and we are fortunate to have had so many citizens give up their lives so we can enjoy its privileges. But freedom is pretty hollow if it produces a 'free for all' and survival of the fittest, as we have seen all too often. We need to honor the legacy of those who have sacrificed by ensuring that freedom provides us with the opportunity to live for the greater good.

NOTES

1. Gould, Stephen J. *Ever Since Darwin*. New York: Norton, 1992, chapter 18.

2. Tocqueville, Alexis de. *Democracy in America, vol.2.* Chicago: UChicago Press, 2000, p.501.

3. Cowen, Tyler. The Loose Reins on U.S. Teenagers Can Produce Trouble or Entrepreneurs. *The New York Times,* June 14, 2007, p. C3.

4. Winthrop, John. *A Modell of Christian Charity*. 1630. On line at http;//history.hanover.edu/texts/winthmod.html.

5. McCarty, Osceola. Quoted in a press release of the University of Southern Mississippi, July 1995. On line at www.pr.usm.edu/oola1.html.

6. King, Martin Luther. text on line at www.usconstitution.net/dream

7. Landsburg, Steven. A Brief History of Economic Time. *The Wall Street Journal,* June 9/10, 2007, p.A8.

8. Brooks,David. A Reality-Based Economy. *The New York Times,* July 24, 2007, p.A23.

9. Bai, Matt. The Poverty Platform. The *New York Times Magazine,* June 10, 2007, p.69.

10. U.S. Census Bureau. On line at www.census.gov/Press-Release/ www/releases/archives/education/007660.html.

11. Dunleavy, M.P. Finding Happiness in the Pursuit. *The New York Times*, June 17, 2007, p. B6.

12. Swartz, Mimi. Shop Stewards on Fantasy Island. *The New York Times Magazine*, June 10, 2007, pp.58–64. (See also Alesina, DiTella and McCullough. *Inequality and Happiness*. Cited by Gaudiani, Claire. *The Greater Good.* New York:Times Books/ Henry Holt, 2003, pp.138/40).

13. *Why Good Things Happen to Good People.* New York: Random House, 2007.

14. Reported by Dr. Robert Emmons of UC Davis, see www.psychology.ucdavis.edu/labs/emmons. Additional information at www.templeton.org/humbleapproach/gratitude

15. www.thanksgiving.org

ADDITIONAL PRINT RESOURCES

Bremner, Robert H. *American Philanthropy*. Chicago: University of Chicago Press, second edition, 1988.
    Bremner provides a broad, readable history of philanthropy tied to key periods in the life of our nation.

Gary, Tracy. *Inspired Philanthropy*. New York: Wiley and Sons, second edition, 2004.
    Gary offers personal and practical advice for leading a generous life.

Gaudiani, Claire. *The Greater Good*. New York: Henry Holt, 2003.
    My research on the relationship of philanthropy to America's economic and social success. Lots of stories.

Lawson, Douglas. *More Give to Live*. San Diego, CA: ALTI Publishing,1999.
    Lawson has basic guidance on tools for giving and a good chapter on the health benefits of philanthropy.

Rosenberg, Claude. *Wealthy and Wise*. New York: Little Brown, 1994.
    Rosenberg is a professional investor/money manager who shows you how to get the most out of your giving.

Salamon, Julie. *Rambam's Ladder*. New York: Workman Publishing, 2003.

This little book is a wonderful meditation on Maimonides' teachings with many contemporary references.

ABOUT THE AUTHORS

Claire Gaudiani (www.clairegaudiani.com) is an expert on the history and economics of American philanthropy. She is clinical professor at New York University, where she directs the graduate program in philanthropic studies.

Gaudiani served for 13 years as President of Connecticut College. She is a Fellow of the American Academy of Arts and Sciences, a director of The Henry Luce Foundation, MBIA Inc., and The National Council for Economic Education. She is a trustee of Worcester Polytechnic Institute.

She holds a PhD in French literature from Indiana University. In addition to *The Greater Good,* she has authored five books and hundreds of articles on topics ranging from foreign language pedagogy to the role of corporate directors.

David Burnett retired from Pfizer, Inc as head of education for Research and Development. Previously he was Associate Dean of Arts and Sciences at the University of Pennsylvania and Associate Professor of Romance Languages. He holds a BA from Princeton University and a PhD, in French literature, from Indiana University.

Gaudiani and Burnett are principals in Gaudiani Associates LLC which provides research, workshops, and philanthropic consulting services to organizations and individuals. They have been married for forty years and have two married children, one granddaughter, and an additional grandchild on the way.

978-0-595-47128-7
0-595-47128-5